www.finishinglinepress.com

Time and Place

*A Year's Worth of Musings
from Gray Horse Ranch*

poems by

Lauren de Vore

Finishing Line Press
Georgetown, Kentucky

Time and Place

*A Year's Worth of Musings
from Gray Horse Ranch*

ACKNOWLEDGMENTS

I am grateful beyond measure to my mother Ruth P. Yaffe and my grandmother
Cleo de Vore Powers for introducing me to the joy of words, to my writing
partner Daniel R. Sapone for years of writerly critique, encouragement and
friendship, and to my husband Paul J. Jackson for loving Gray Horse Ranch
as much as I do and for his patience and understanding when I disappear for
hours or days a-horseback or into the vagaries of literary muse.

Publisher: Leah Maines
Editor: Christen Kincaid
Cover Art: Paul J. Jackson
Author Photo: Paul J. Jackson
Cover Design: Kitty Madison

Printed in the USA on acid-free paper.
Order online: www.finishinglinepress.com
            also available on amazon.com

Author inquiries and mail orders:
Finishing Line Press
P. O. Box 1626
Georgetown, Kentucky 40324
U. S. A.

Table of Contents

Sonnets for the Twenty-First Century

Most of us learned about sonnets in high school as a poetical form that originated in thirteenth-century Italy. The form became a staple for poets like Dante Alighieri (1265–1321) and Guido Cavalcanti (c. 1250–1300) and was made most famous by Francesco Petrarca (1304–1374) and William Shakespeare (c. 1564–1616). As exemplified by Petrarch and Shakespeare, the sonnet is a two-part, fourteen-line poem that presents an argument of some sort. The first eight lines (two quatrains) advance a proposition, problem, or question, and the remaining six lines (quatrain and couplet) propose a resolution or answer. The final couplet serves as the punch line, driving home the poet's conclusion.

Although the form has seen a variety of rhyme schemes, a traditional Petrarchan sonnet uses an "abba abba cdcd cd" pattern, and a Shakespearean sonnet typically uses either an "abba cddc effe gg" or an "abab cdcd efef gg" rhyming scheme. One of the most distinctive features of a sonnet is its rhythm, arising from the use of iambic pentameter. Each line contains five "iambs," pairs of syllables consisting of one unstressed syllable followed by a stressed syllable (e.g., "alone again, I cry myself to sleep").

The sonnet has endured through the centuries as an iconic poetic form. One of the most enduring poems in American history, engraved at the base of the Statue of Liberty to welcome immigrants to America, is a Petrarchan sonnet.

The New Colossus, by Emma Lazarus

Not like the brazen giant of Greek fame,
With conquering limbs astride from land to land;
Here at our sea-washed, sunset gates shall stand
A mighty woman with a torch, whose flame
Is the imprisoned lightning, and her name
Mother of Exiles. From her beacon-hand
Glows world-wide welcome; her mild eyes command
The air-bridged harbor that twin cities frame.
"Keep, ancient lands, your storied pomp!" cries she
With silent lips. "Give me your tired, your poor,
Your huddled masses yearning to breathe free,
The wretched refuse of your teeming shore.
Send these, the homeless, tempest-tost to me,
I lift my lamp beside the golden door!"

Much poetry in the latter half of the twentieth century drifted away from formal structure and strict rhyme, opting instead for varied line lengths, natural rhythms, and looser rhymes. Often called "free verse," this approach found widespread use in song lyrics for popular music. Quite a debate erupted in literary circles, however, with some songwriters and poets arguing that formal poetical forms limited their creativity and narrowed their ability to appeal to a wider audience. Others countered that, for the serious creative, precision in rhythm and rhyme need not restrict artistic expression. T.S. Eliot famously asserted, "No verse is free for the poet who wants to do a good job." Certainly, nobody can argue that the sonnet form inhibited Robert Frost from the heights of creative expression. In the poem below, he clearly demonstrates that the sonnet allows more-than-ample flexibility to reveal the truths of the ages.

The Oven Bird, by Robert Frost

There is a singer everyone has heard,
Loud, a mid-summer and a mid-wood bird,
Who makes the solid tree trunks sound again.
He says that leaves are old and that for flowers
Mid-summer is to spring as one to ten.
He says the early petal-fall is past
When pear and cherry bloom went down in showers
On sunny days a moment overcast;
And comes that other fall we name the fall.
He says the highway dust is over all.
The bird would cease and be as other birds
But that he knows in singing not to sing.
The question that he frames in all but words
Is what to make of a diminished thing.

So, can working within a clearly defined poetical form free the imagination? Can structure imposed on the art form help poets tap into what's raw and exciting in their writing? Can imagery and emotion be compellingly conveyed in fourteen rhyming lines of iambic pentameter? Seven centuries of the most widely read and revered poets have answered these questions with a resounding "Yes."

Indeed, the twenty-first century's "twitter culture" would seem to be ripe for a renaissance of sonnets. The appeal of telling stories in one hundred and forty syllables can be irresistible.

Tweets Poetical, by Lauren de Vore

Some say the sonnet is outdated verse,
Sententious and obscure, archaic with
It's prejudice 'gainst feet trochaic, curse
Of students forced to parse the poet's pith.

And yet a sonnet's just a rhyming tweet,
One hundred forty syllables is all,
Three quatrains and a couplet short and sweet,
Profane, profound or scribbling on a wall.

Like anything with rules, within them it's
A free-for-all. The art is knowing when
And where to bend the rules as best befits
The poet's vision and the poem's zen.

So grab your tablets, all you twitter hawks,
Tweet sonnets from the subways and sidewalks.

In this volume of decidedly twenty-first-century verse, Lauren de Vore demonstrates the creativity possible with this enduring form of poetic expression. What we see in this collection of sonnets is the achievement of goals any artist would proudly pursue—the illumination of fundamental themes of human existence as experienced in a certain place and time—specifically, a small ranch in the hills of northern California.

Note that this is not a book to zip through. It is best read a few sonnets at a time, leisurely, taking the time to roll your mouth around the words, to savor the imagery and storytelling and allow them to seep into your imagination. Like old friends, the poems have more to offer as they expand and interconnect with repeated readings, repeated visits. So, settle back in a comfy chair, relax, and time-travel through a year at Gray Horse Ranch.

Enjoy,

—Daniel R. Sapone

Dan Sapone participates with Lauren in a small writing group in the Tri-Valley of northern California. An experienced literary educator and dramatist, Dan recently retired from a long career as an editor/writer. He writes short fiction and nonfiction, and is currently deep into the writing of his first novel.

A Poet's Prosing

Obsession with time and place is a human universal. In one way or another, we all ask why we're here, wherever here is, and we try to find the place...a place, any place...where we belong. Likewise, we continually mark the passage of time and lament its too-rapid progress and our own squandering of precious moments.

Having lost my father when I was a young child, I am particularly sensitive to the fleeting-ness of time and the ephemerality of life.

Gift

Why am I so obsessed with time, you ask,
For does it not stretch to eternity?
So thought I once, till fate in death's own mask
Did disabuse me of such certainty.

For when I was but six, my father died,
And with the loss I learned that time is gift,
Not guarantee, that some are richly plied
While others just as worthy get short shrift.

My father surely thought he'd ample time
For all the hopes and dreams a life should hold,
And yet he died while barely in his prime—
Down payment for a daughter's growing old.

Knowing that time's a gift that can't be bought,
I treasure every day that he had not.

The poems in this collection are musings on the passing of a year at Gray Horse Ranch, my handful of acres in the hills east of San Francisco Bay. They are an attempt to put into words what I so love about this place—the living close to the land, by nature's rules, not man's. The solitude amidst teeming life, the peace and quiet that hums with energy, the timelessness and the constant change. In touch with the eons-old rhythms of the natural world, I gain insights unavailable in a city setting into man's place, my place, in today's world.

With every dawn, every sunset, every first bud of spring and last lingering leaf of autumn, with every glimpse of something new or unexpected, I am one of the lucky ones to have found my place.

—Lauren de Vore

PLACE AND TIME

This Patch of Earth

What is it 'bout a place, a certain patch
Of earth and sky that signals this is home?
Is it the sapphire sky no gem can match,
The sweep of golden hills I long to roam?

Is it th'extravagance of stars that fill
The night, the fields with horses running free,
Perhaps the redtail's cry or lark's sweet trill?
'Tis all of this and more that's home for me.

Around the world I've roamed to places so
Spectacular they took my breath away,
And yet without a pause I've turned to go
When home called out; I could not stay away.

Restless I wandered till at last I found
This patch of earth and sky to which I'm bound.

A Lavish Stretch of Time

How is it that a year viewed in advance
Seems such a lavish stretch of time, more than
Enough for every project, scheme, and plan
With which to fill calendrical expanse?

In hindsight though, a dozen months fly by
In just a flash. 'Twas only yesterday
That spring lay soft upon the land; today
The winter's chill embrittles earth and sky.

No matter how much time I have, 'tis ne'er
Enough. E'en at the close of longest day,
There's always something more to do or say,
For endings ever take me unaware.

Yet every ending's dawn to something new
As years and lives spin out in endless queue.

That Rarest of Things

I've horse spit on my face and horse #*&! on
My boots, my hair is flecked with something green,
I ache as if I've run a marathon,
But I don't mind—I've got the equine gene!

To me, horse sweat is sweeter than perfume
And nickers more addicting than a drug,
And if I'm out of sorts or sunk in gloom,
The cure is simple—give a horse a hug.

Such joy, such bliss to ride, to fly as one
Across the hills or amble 'long a creek,
And then in silence stand when day is done,
For 'twixt us two there is no need to speak.

I've found with horses that rarest of things—
A love that loves despite all shortcomings.

Autumn

The Summer Child's Lament

September is the saddest month of all,
For though the glow of summer lingers on,
A certain cast of light at dusk and dawn
Betrays the all-too-near approach of fall.

And I, a summer child, turn softly sad
As days grow short and mares' tails streak on high.
Though other folk revive when autumn's nigh,
Myself I'm conscious of the loss, not glad.

For once again the days have slipped away.
So many plans I had but few are done,
For I, grasshopper-like, the morrow shunned
To revel in the sun and seize the day.

So fine the summer was yet now it fades,
And over all a wistfulness pervades.

Autumn Fugue

The autumn is austere in my home hills,
No gaudy trees of scarlet, orange and gold
That shout "fall's here!" in palettes overbold
Like partyers bedecked in flame-bright frills.

My hills are tawny now, the grass once gilt
Is brittle straw, the oaks are veiled with dust.
Hawks circle high above as sharp-edged gusts
Ensummon clouds that stream like watery milk.

Though sleepy outward, deep a current thrums
In rock and log and hidden earthen lair.
The voices may be hushed, yet everywhere
A pulsing fugue of vibrant life force hums.

Th'expectant land abides for season's turn,
All senses keyed for hint of rain's return.

Taking Stock

October is my time to introspect,
As like a gleaner following the scythe
I cull through recollection's field and, eyes
Attuned to see, unflinchingly reflect.

It's easy to tot up the obvious,
That never-ending list of tasks that should
Be done before the rains arrive and would
Were I, in this, not kin to Sisyphus.

Th'intangibles are harder to appraise;
Did I come through for those who needed me?
Did kindness guide my words and honesty
My acts, or did I tread a selfish maze?

One must at times take candid look within
In striving for a life that's genuine.

First Rain

The first rain of the season fell today.
'Twas just a shower, barely more than mist,
As raindrops like a lover gently kissed
The parchéd land 'fore trickling away.

So notable the first rain of the fall,
Yet when the summer's searing hot, in vain
I try but can't remember spring's last rain—
Was it a drench or just a passing squall?

Why do, in memory, the "firsts" hold sway?
So often it's the "lasts" I would recall—
That smile, hug, laugh, kiss, step, word, breath—so small
And unremarked that day, they slipped away.

How could I've known back then, back yesterday,
Those were the memories I'd want today?

Dark Chocolate

November is like chocolate, a blend
Of dark and light, the bitter and the sweet.
The days are short with winter round the bend,
And rain that finally falls is welcome treat.

The thirsty land imbibes till it can hold
No more, and excess turns my fields to bog.
Although I hate the mud, I am consoled
That winter storms perforce are spring's prologue.

'Tis unavoidable that seasons turn,
And dark and dreary times succeed the gay.
And while I dread the cold, I shall not spurn
The storms but look for grace amidst the gray.

The finest chocolate is bittersweet;
So is the life that's fully lived, complete.

Turkey Day

What is this now—some sort of turkey fest?
I'm overrun with fowl, with scads of birds
Parading 'round my garden like they're guests,
Just pleased as punch t'escape the day's hazards,

That day where every turkey fears to end
Up as the main course 'stead of company.
I too have gathered family and friends
To share a day of feast and bonhomie,

A day of too much football, too much wine,
And when, at last, the clove-stuck ham is served,
We offer thanks for tasty toothsome swine.

I see by beady eyes our meal's observed
Although on turkey bird we do not dine,
But touch my flow'rs, and you'll be what I serve!

WINTER

Nostalgia-ncy

December is a time for fantasy,
A time to recreate the favorite parts
Of childhood and reminisce to hearts'
Content with unabashed nostalgia-ncy.

As soon as there's a nip in air, a yen
Comes over me for gingersnaps and hot
Mulled wine, for Christmas gifts that aren't store-bought,
For midnight carols, sleigh rides and snowmen.

All this despite the fact I hate the cold
And always sing off key. But still I love
The holidays with shining star and dove
Of peace and other symbols ageless old.

For now, reality I will eschew;
Let faith in goodness, hope and joy renew.

The Cold Short Days

The cold short days of winter hold a wealth
Of subtle beauty waiting patiently
For those who walk the land in gentle stealth
With senses tuned to hear and scent and see.

A cast of gilded lavender comes o'er
The sky when storm is brewing in the west.
An ozone tang precedes the night's downpour,
And wind-blown descants stir, then soothe my rest.

Come morn, the mist gives way to crisp bright light
That carves the hillside shadows knife-edge sharp.
My rain-soaked pastures shimmer crystal white
As unseen birdsong rings like silver harp.

Though wintertime is drear, still beauty thrives;
Though storms assault, the fragile soul survives.

Scribe a New Slate

A welcome respite January brings,
A lull 'twixt holidays and spring's return
In which to contemplate the offerings
The new year holds in its twelve-month sojourn.

Such joy to scribe upon a fresh clean slate
As yet unmarred by blot or smear, with chance
To start anew, to change, to set things straight,
To aim and not just cede to circumstance.

So what to write, what story do I tell?
For at year's end, that which I most will rue
Is not what's done, regardless what befell,
But what, whate'er th'excuse, I didn't do.

Each year's a gift, and better is to try
And fail, than fearing failure fail to try.

By the Fireside

Ensconced in favorite chair by fireside,
Absorbing book and lazy cat collude
To banish consciousness of time and tide
And give excuse for welcome solitude.

The winter's freezing grip on copse and field
Drives creatures all to sanctuary deep.
In dens and nests and burrows by the weald,
The furred and feathered silent vigil keep.

And I asylum find in lamp-lit hall
With fire in hearth, a kettle on for tea
And chosen book at hand. Once in the thrall
Of printed page, the storm's but memory.

A gift this unplanned idleness, with none
To please but self till ice give way to sun.

Out from In

At kitchen sink I stand and watch the storm
Assail my garden and the fields beyond,
And with a force primordial transform
Their man-made order to chaotic pond.

Against my house the elements collide
As if to vanquish it and all within,
But sturdy roof and steadfast walls divide
The raging storm from calm, the out from in.

'Tis natural I suppose the world to see
As either-or, as wild or tame, as black or white
And known or not, and then so easily
To us or them and thereby wrong or right.

In life, as storm, we cleave to "in," with stout
Defenses raised against the fearsome "out."

Seduction

A fickle month is February for
It's neither fully winter nor the spring.
And so the seasons joust with storms that roar
And lambent sun that blunts the icy sting.

And like the belle who's alternately wooed
Then spurned, each sunny day seduces me
With vernal hopes, till wind and rain so rude-
-ly douse those dreams with chill reality.

You'd think I'd learn that winter never cedes
The field without a fight. 'Tis foolishness,
I know, to hang my hopes on fragile reeds
Like spring and sun but do so nonetheless.

Though fickle weather, captious fate assault,
Hope springs eternal, hopeful to a fault.

Spring

Groundhog Days

My cabin-fevered spirits rise and fall
With barometric synchronicity,
For I'm fed up with domesticity
And thoughts of further indoor tasks appall.

I've sorted socks and burnished locks, I've cleaned
And polished, mended, tended, organized
And scads of stuff on eBay advertised—
Much more of this, I should be quarantined!

Like Punxsutawney Phil, I poke my head
Out periodically to scan for signs
Of early spring. And when there's none, I whine
That I, like he, should just go back to bed.

Although I fret that winter ne'er will go,
I know it will—the groundhog told me so.

The Sought Is Found

March brings me down to earth and coldly shows
Me once again that though I long for spring,
The wintertide must run its course and knows
Nor cares but naught for mortal daydreaming.

The hills are patient, stoical, but I
Have not their luxury of time. I range
From windswept ridge to sheltered vale to spy
Some trace, some secret sign of season's change.

Downcast my rambling quest has had no luck,
I head for home through sodden fields of mud
Where grass should grow, when there amidst the muck
And mire are golden buttercups in bud.

So oft what's sought I've found in plainest view
Once from determined search my eye withdrew.

Spring Palette

I woke today to find that spring has sprung,
As in the night, it seems, the constant hills
Have shed their tattered rags and faded frills
And over all a fresh green mantle flung.

And not just green but every verdant shade,
From newest leaf that's almost gold to oak
So deep it's nearly black. No artist's stroke
Can render even half the hues arrayed.

And even if some artist could, no art
Can capture that rare mix of song and scent
That's spring—duet of lark and frog, ferment
Of earth and log—the sum transcends the part.

Man's art, though great, is but a shadow faint
In light of what the hands of nature paint.

Festival

April's a-hum with energy, a zest
That manifests in every leaf and flower,
In every chirp and trill, intent to wrest
The fullest measure from each golden hour.

My spirits cramped by winter cold unfurl
Like petals tightly held in bud released
At last t'embrace the sun. With glee I hurl
Myself into a whirl of life new-leased.

I'm filled with plans for long, luxurious days
Ahead, far more than I can hope t'achieve,
But from spring's vantage point, the view o'ersways
My common sense and dreams anew I weave.

With spring the world revives, exuberant,
And I join in, a joyful celebrant.

A Greater Magic

The alchemy of May transfigures hills
Of grass to gold, a shining backdrop for
A magic greater still as life refills
The coffers 'minished by the year before.

The little doe that lives amidst my oaks
Had twins this year, the wily turkey hen
Has hatched her brood, and soon my mare will coax
Her newborn foal to try to rise again.

So placid and serene, the mare, the doe,
The hen. Do they not grasp the miracle
Of which they're part, or do perhaps they know
What lies beyond the inexplicable?

Of all the mysteries one can behold,
None's greater than new life succeeding old.

Standing at the Pasture Gate

Eyes closed and nose to tail, my horses doze
Atop a hill where breezes blow the flies
Away and thin the redtail's piercing cries
That else might jar their afternoon repose.

I'd thought to bring them to the barn, to brush
Them, give them treats, perhaps to saddle one,
For it's a perfect day to ride—the sun
Warm on my back, the hillsides gold and lush.

Yet standing at the pasture gate, I've not
The heart to interrupt their nap; t'would be
Pure selfishness t'insist they rouse for me.

The bond 'tween horse and man cannot be bought
Or bartered for a scoop of grain or flake
Of hay. It's theirs to give, not mine to take.

Summer

Turn Back the Clock

June's heat sets air and dust to shimmering
In light so bright that color fades to black
And white, and through photonic sleight turns back
The clock t'when joy was found in simple things.

A tree to climb, a creek t'explore, a kite
To fly, or p'raps to ramble aimlessly
With fellow knee-skinned cohorts just to see
What's to be seen till suppertime's in sight.

Though it's been years since I was climbing trees,
The lustrous days of June awake the child
In me, and for a spell I am beguiled
To slow my steps and savor summer's ease.

Reminded I am yet again—the best
Pleasures are those that are the simplest.

The Horse Chestnut Tree

A hint of grape and lilac wafts from o'er
The hill where grows th'horse chestnut tree,
A tree to me that's perfect metaphor
For summertime's ephemerality.

The last to bloom and first to fade, yet in
Its prime incomparable, so sweet its flowers
And opulent its crown. It's ever been
A favorite tree, though few its glory hours.

'Tis surely one of nature's ironies—
The more splendid, the shorter reign is giv'n.
Seasons and lives all have their expiries,
And in their passing hearts are rent and riv'n.

And yet the chestnut tree marks not the hours
But simply shares the beauty of its flowers.

Growing Gray

At birth, he wore a coal black coat and three
White socks, though lighter haloes round his eyes
Foretold his formal dress was but disguise
And black would turn to gray eventually.

The years rolled by and sure enough, before
Me stood some sixteen hands of gorgeous gray,
His mane and tail agleam like silver spray.
As much my dark-hued colt I did adore,

I think him far more beautiful now grown
And gray. Would that these self-same eyes could see
My own hair gray and prize it 'ccordingly;
Instead I see the mark of nascent crone.

I wonder what my handsome horse would say.
Does he think me more lovely now I'm gray?

Beach Boardwalk

July's what summer's all about, with hand-
Cranked ice cream, carnivals and fireworks
Rekindling youthful faith that life is grand,
That round each corner something wondrous lurks.

In endless possibility believed
I once, before reality broke down
The walls of innocence. Bereaved, deceived,
T'were easy to submerge in gloom and drown.

But somewhere 'long the line, I chose to say
"If I can't have the whole loaf, I'll have half."
As summer's warmth keeps winter's chill at bay,
So tears hold off so long as I can laugh.

With rollercoasters, swings, a carousel,
Life is the grandest game, and ain't it swell!

While Summer's Fine

Come August I'm caught in a tug-of-war
'Twixt plans I made in spring so purposely
And spur-of-moment caprice to ignore
Those best-laid schemes and simply carpé di.

The summer days are long and I have much
To do—fences to mend and garden tend,
Preserves to make and fields to rake, oh such
A list of projects 'fore the season's end.

Yet summertime is short and there is much
That I must do—roses to smell, sweet wine
To taste, a lover's cherished face to touch,
So many joys to seize while summer's fine.

Oh what to do, the balance must be weighed,
For wine will sour and love like roses fade.

Parting Day

The doe whose fawn clung to her side's alone
And single now, so too the turkey hen.
Empty the redtail's nest, the fox's den
Now kits are grown and nestlings fledged and flown.

Year after year, the babes are born. They're fed
And nurtured, kept from harm…and then they're gone.
And left behind are mothers who, each dawn
And dusk, face empty nest and empty bed.

How fare they on their own again? Are they
Relieved their mothering work for now is done
Or grieved o'er absent daughter, absent son?

Though nothing can forestall the parting day,
How do they bear each year from babes to part?
Just one child's leaving nearly broke my heart.

Time and Place

A Year's Worth

A year seems such a vast expanse of time,
Three hundred sixty days and more as earth
Wheels 'round the sun, a dozen months for mirth
And love and tears, for tempests and sunshine.

Such plans I made to fill my days, but oft
They're merely tracings in the sand. For just
A puff of fate can turn them all to dust
As onto new and different paths I'm tossed.

And truth be told, it is these times when o'er
An unexpected peak I've climbed or 'round
A hidden corner turned, I've wisdom found
And lessons learned that I'd not gained before.

There is a lifetime, more, within each year,
Replete with all that's joyful, rueful, dear.

Country Calling

The country calls but to a few, to those
Who prize the storms as much the gentle days
And count as wealth not stock portfolios
But every subtle dawn and sunset blaze,

To those who mark the seasons, not the hours,
And know that land's not owned but held in trust,
Who midst a field o'ergrown see first the flowers,
Treasuring the beauty sprung from lowly dust.

It calls to those who grudge not days of toil
Nor tithe of sweat and blood, who feel within
Each silent stone and hefted clump of soil
The pulse of all to come and all that's been.

The country called and I, my spirit stirred.
The country called and I, thank god, I heard.

What Think...

What think the dragonflies that hatch and die
Before the dandelions turn to fluff,
Before the fledgling hawks take to the sky?
Think they the time they have is time enough?

What of the hills and mountain peaks, what think
They as they watch the noble buck collapse
And breathe its last where late it stood to drink,
As primal plains are littered with life's scraps?

Think they that having stood for eons they're
Immune to time, or do they watch their own
Demise, slopes crumbled, stripped of verdant hair,
Reduced to dust from which all life has flown?

I think I'd rather be the dragonfly
Than live to watch the world grow old and die.

Atop the Cloud-Kissed Knoll

Bury me please atop the knoll, the cloud-
Kissed one my horses love; no coffin box
To seal me in, just earth and grass as shroud
And for a marker nothing more than rocks.

In silent wakefulness, let me look out
Upon these hills and fields so dear to me;
Let daisies, buttercups and poppies sprout
To carpet me in rainbow tapestry.

Let me taste midnight sky and golden morn,
Let me hear star song in each drop of rain,
Let me see children of my children born,
Each one a link in time's unending chain.

In life these hills did hold my heart, so let
Me lie in theirs until the last sun sets.